Journey of Rediscovery

Leanne Michelle

Journey of Rediscovery © 2022 Leanne Michelle

All rights reserved.

Presentation by *BookLeaf Publishing*

Web: www.bookleafpub.com

E-mail: info@bookleafpub.com

ISBN: 9789357692335

First edition 2022

Written with love for Andrew and Maxwell.

I love you both more than all the moons and stars in the sky, always.

ACKNOWLEDGEMENT

Thank you to my partner, family and friends who all believed in me on the days I was unable to believe in myself. Lots of love to you all.

Thank you to the emergency services personnel who attended my home to administer life saving care and the staff at The Prince Charles Hospital for helping me save my life. Special mention to the staff at The Prince Charles Hospital Mental Health Ward - East Wing, who cared for me when I needed it most. You guys are all amazing; each of you are heroes.

Gypsy-Rose/Gyps/Cherie - thank you for taking me under your wing on the ward. I wish you endless love and healing and I hope you find in your life what you are searching for.

To the survivors of attempted suicide - keep fighting. You've got this. I believe in you.

To the families who lost loved ones to this awful illness - please take care of one another.

To those who are now angels, we are always loving you. Your presence and your heart remains eternally with your loved ones.

PREFACE

Journey of Rediscovery was birthed as an explorative piece into my heart, mind and imagination.. There is a mix of personal poetry drawing on life experience while exploring the disclarity of Post Natal Depression.

A mixture of realism and imagination, Journey of Rediscovery is sure to set your heart alight as you absorb the raw honesty of each piece herein.

I have written a lot of my mental health and as a survivor of suicide. I want to normalise conversations around mental health. The Mental Health system in Australia is dangerously underfunded, dangerously under resourced and dangerously under pressure. If nothing else, I hope my writing helps someone else heal. The time to normalise these conversations and draw attention to an almost broken and struggling system is now.

All poems are published in the order in which I wrote them.

Morning Brew

On waking I seek
The sweet elixir of life;
Delicious coffee.

I Am.

"Post Natal Depression",
The Psychiatrist said.
A knife to the heart;
Tears, I shed.

"Look on the bright side",
Said the ones I love.
I try; the answers I seek
Are not above.

"Don't dwell on things",
Said well meaning friends.
When the demons grasp you,
All you want is an end.

You consider pills.
You consider blades.
Day by day,
Your life force fades.

Dreaming of an end,
Wondering "what will be?"
Then I remember -
It's you and me.

I need to keep swimming;
I need to stay afloat.
My son and my husband
Are my lifeboat.

When the seas are rough
And the riptide swallows me -
Husband, hold out your hand.
Help, set me free.

Freedom from suffering.
Not freedom from life.
I am needed here;
I am Mother. I am Wife.

My Son

My son.
Forever love.
Always deep in my heart.
Your smile lights up the darkest of days;
Sunshine.

Your touch;
You gift comfort.
Your scent I breathe deeply.
You are protector from the dark;
Safety.

Your laugh.
You are music.
Your giggle gives me life.
Your innocence is my safety;
True love.

Embrace.
Holding you close.
Your love I always crave.
I love you more than all the stars
And moons.

Your eyes.

Always shining.
Forever smiling bright.
You give me light; caught in the dark.
Bright sky.

My son.
You gift comfort.
Your giggle gives me life.
I love you more than all the stars,
Bright Sky.

Sunflowers

Into the room I walked.
I was nervous, I was scared;
Deep down I knew
Together we'd heal as we talked.

For weeks we met
In that one room.
Talking and healing,
A time we must not forget.

We each shine bright.
We are strong. We are brave.
Together in the same garden
We seek sunshine's light.

Sunflowers, each of us are.
No matter what we're doing,
Sunflowers by day and by night
A bright star.

Forever we will bloom.
I am eternally grateful
I put my fear aside
And walked into that room.

No matter how near or far,
Together we are always bonded.
I love you, my Sunflowers.
You know who you are.

Trapped

There's a whirlpool inside my head
Swirling and spinning so fast.
I don't know which thought to free.
The spinning makes me feel ill;
Meditation doesn't help. What I seek? A pill.

The meds bring me shame.
They make me feel "less than".
Without them, I feel I have no name.
The meds are not forever, training wheels in
fact.
The day will come when I am strong;
My thought processes clear and intact.

Poetry about mental illness I did not wish to
write.
But you, dear reader, are closer than you think.
We are all out here, hiding in plain sight.

So please, always be kind.
Many of us carry so much hurt;
For we are trapped in our mind.

Valium

The voices. Oh so loud.
One pill. Serenity. Peace.
Quiet. Still. Calm. Hope.

Andrew

I really thought you didn't exist.
Too good to be true. Not real.
Chasing my dream, I chose to persist.
When we connected my heart you did steal.

Imagine my surprise when we first met.
My beating heart so loud, it vibrated sound.
Our first kiss magical; I will not forget.
Even today, you make my heart pound.

A home together we have created.
A life of love and dreams we have made.
So many fun memories when we dated.
Our laughter will never fade.

I love you, my sweet Andrew.
Every day, without a doubt, I choose you.

Magpie

Pen to paper, I sit and think.
No words are coming. It stinks!
I look to the birds as they fly.
Still, the words have run dry.
The Magpie's beautiful song he sings.
Maybe some meal worms to them I will bring.
Suddenly an entire flock arrives.
I cannot believe it - in front of my eyes!
Fledglings, adolescents and even old greys,
Their song and their beauty truly makes my day.
The beautiful Magpie, so misunderstood.
I love my Magpie family, here in our
neighbourhood.
Each day I listen for them to sing.
When I hear them I know -
Happiness, my day will bring.

Sleep, Sweet Boy

My sweet little boy, why won't you sleep?
Your nightlight, warm; loving; secure.
Your lullaby softly sung.
My gentle touch, soothing.
My embrace, calming.
Holding you close.
Dreams await,
Sweet boy.
Sleep.

Whispering Wind

Wind.
Blustery. Brisk.
Howling. Swaying. Moving.
What do you whisper?
Wisdom.

Kooki

At my former home you'd appear.
First just you and then another would come.
Always you'd bring laughter and fun.
My favourite days? When you were near.

Two. Then three. Then four.
Before I knew it, you'd bring many.
You would all come. You'd visit me.
When I thought I knew your riot, you would
bring more.

Now no longer in that home
The visits from your riot I miss.
Life without you, Kooki, has little bliss.
I think of you daily; I hope you're not alone.

No matter where you are, my Kookaburra
friends -
In my heart you always have a home.

Full Moon

Outside I stood,
Feet dirty and bare.
Up at you I looked.
Opened my heart and stared.

My crystals on display.
My decks under your clear light.
Gratitude to the Universe I expressed
On a clear and starry night.

I widened my arms, opened my heart.
Bent down, palms to Earth.
I sought your love and protection,
To those within my hearth.

Up I stood.
To you I prayed.
Sharing all my wishes;
Manifestations made.

Grandmother Moon and Grandfather Sky,
Ancient wisdom unlocked.
Freedom you gifted me -
My spirituality no longer blocked.

The possibilities are endless
And for that I thank you.
Until next we meet,
Feminine Full Moon,
I bid you "adieu".

Hope

Today the voices were quiet.
To me that was weird.
So used to noise in my head,
Sanity I feared.

The hallucinations -
There was but one.
With it I fought.
It was me who won!

Today I had energy.
I felt good. Even anew!
Was today a dream?
Too good to be true?

Hope is the answer.
Hope is the key.
Hope I will hold.
Hope will set me free.

Normalise, I must

Hazy and head pounding, here I sit.
Machines beeping and buzzing
Clearly the dose not a big enough hit.
"Fuck you, brain", I keep cussing.

I don't know what came over me.
Was it depression? Anxiety? Stress?
The answers I cannot yet see.
Trapped in my head - I feel like a mess.

End my pain, oh how I tried.
All the blades blunt and weak.
It was pills and liquor, while I cried.
Finally I collapsed. Life felt bleak.

Vague recollections with whom I spoke;
The police arrived, laid me on my side.
Refusing my freedom, they wouldn't let me
choke.
They made me breathe and now I want to hide.

Normalise these conversations I must.
I survived suicide. Only just.

The Ward

Not where I expected to be.
Cold. Clinical. Out of key.
In the admission suite I cried,
Realising - I had almost died.

A short stay there I had.
It really wasn't all that bad.
The Nurses, lovely. The patients, kind.
We're all the same - trying to mend our mind.

A catalyst for healing this is.
My son needs a mother - his.
My husband needs his wife.
My ward stay? It saved my life.

Too much stigma around the psych ward.
It is a place of healing, untold magic stored.

If it weren't for the checks, concern and care
My life would be different.
I wouldn't have one to share.

Thank you to the Nurses on the front line.
The Mental Health Ward is one of a kind.
Your dedication on the hardest of days,
You are all heroes in so many ways.

Leela, Shepherd of my Heart

It's true what they say about dogs -
Their love is unconditional.
It's even truer what they say about German
Shepherds -
Their love is like no other.

Loved by four Shepherds, I have been blessed.
Ellie. Logan. Luna. Angels they now are.
Guardians of my heart -
Forever they will remain.

Then there is Leela, as known to me.
"Carefree Delilah" on her pedigree.
Carefree? Absolutely she is!
Strong and bold like Delilah? I'd expect no less.

Leela has loved me for three years so far.
All over the country we have travelled;
Often beating borders and covid restrictions.
Not by choice and by car.

Everywhere in such a short life we have been.
From the rough side of Melbourne,
To Adelaide, to Whyalla.
Even through the Territory she has seen!

Leela, always ready to celebrate.
Always ready to play.
Watching over me and my family,
Leela constantly radiates love.

You are my German Shepherd,
Keeper of my heart.
I want our days to be long and many,
I never want us to part.
I love you, sweet Leela.

Taylor

The day the news broke...
25th March 2022 was the day.
All my breath left me. I choked.
My heart, shattered. Every which way.

Foo Fighters - more than "just a band".
Taylor, their incredibly talented drummer.
Foo Fighters always gave me a hand,
Especially when life was hard and a real
bummer.

Struggled all this time, I have been.
Listening to their music now hurts.
Without Foo Fighters I no longer feel seen.
I feel for Dave. Now Taylor but first Kurt.

I think the time has come to face the pain.
Listen to the musical love of my life;
To play Foo Fighters once again...
Without Taylor, it cuts like a knife.

An Angel in Heaven you now are.
Taylor, I hope you feel all our love, even from
afar.

Happy Heavenly Birthday

Happy Heavenly Birthday, Dad.
I wonder when you look down what you see.
I miss you so much, I'm trying not to be sad.
I really hope you are proud of me.

Your grandson, oh how you'd love him.
A sense of humour just like yours.
Spontaneous adventures you'd share on a whim.
You'd teach him fishing, woodwork and even
scroll saws.

Today we have seen butterflies;
They remind me you are here.
Today instead of beginning to cry,
I will shed a happy tear.

So many memories we shared when you were
alive.
I can't wait to talk of you to my son
About our time together, Earthside.
As far as dads go, the Jackpot I'd won.

Today is your day, dad. 16 November.
Happy Heavenly Birthday.
I will love you forever and ever.

Nightmares

Why won't the nightmares stop?
People I love getting hurt.
So over the top.
I want a redo, just like Kurt.

The stress of them is too much.
Nightmares so grotesque, so vivid.
Why not dreams of music or similar as such?
My emotions on waking, often scared or livid.

I just want to dream nice dreams.
Of music. Of concerts. Of fun.
My brain won't allow me this, it seems.
Sleep now not a priority - one I want to shun.

My body, it needs to slow down, to rest.
It needs relief from the anxiety.
But my nightmares put me to the test.
They are really bothering me.

Mental unwellness is silent, a constant fight.
If you share your sunshine, survive we just
might.

Query

Two more poems to write.
How will I finish this piece?
Positivity.

My Army

A marathon I did just start.
A journey of healing,
Rebuilding my heart.
So full of feeling...

Search for my "Why" I must.
I am mother. I am wife.
My WHY is my spirit and my trust.
So many reasons to keep my life.

My husband, loving and full of care.
He radiates warmth and light,
A life with him I will share.
By my side and in my army, we fight.

My son, innocent. Sweet.
He is too young, his heart pure.
He loves his mum, his needs I will meet.
In my army he plays a part -
He is the key of my heart.

My family, my brothers, my mum.
Their wives, their sons and daughters.
Strength, I will find some.
They are in my army, ready for slaughter.

My friends, nearest and dearest.
My best friends, the truth they will tell;
Their judgement often the clearest.
My army grows - at dawn, we ring the bell.

I have many reasons WHY in my life.
Many that are my priority, my want, my need.
I'm not to allow my brain to get me into strife.
My army is large, their help I will heed.

I want to live; I don't know what happens now.
My Army; my WHY, are teaching me how.
Pen to paper each night,
Something special I will continue to write.